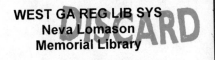

John F. Kennedy

John F. Kennedy

Robert Dallek

OXFORD
UNIVERSITY PRESS

2011

OXFORD
UNIVERSITY PRESS

Oxford University Press, Inc., publishes works that further
Oxford University's objective of excellence
in research, scholarship, and education.

Oxford   New York

Auckland   Cape Town   Dar es Salaam   Hong Kong   Karachi
Kuala Lumpur   Madrid   Melbourne   Mexico City   Nairobi
New Delhi   Shanghai   Taipei   Toronto

With offices in

Argentina   Austria   Brazil   Chile   Czech Republic   France   Greece
Guatemala   Hungary   Italy   Japan   Poland   Portugal   Singapore
South Korea   Switzerland   Thailand   Turkey   Ukraine   Vietnam

Published by Oxford University Press, Inc.
198 Madison Avenue, New York, New York 10016

www.oup.com

Oxford is a registered trademark of Oxford University Press

Library of Congress Cataloging-in-Publication Data
Dallek, Robert.
John F. Kennedy / Robert Dallek.
p. cm.
Includes bibliographical references.
ISBN 978-0-19-975436-6 (hardcover : alk. paper)
1. Kennedy, John F. (John Fitzgerald), 1917–1963.   2. Presidents—United States—Biography.
I. Dallek, Robert. Unfinished life.   II. Title.
E842.D28 2011
973.922092—dc22 [B]   2010032397

1 3 5 7 9 8 6 4 2
Printed in the United States of America
on acid-free paper

John F. Kennedy

Preface

It is a common saying among historians that you write a book to forget a subject. In practice, however, it is not so easy: For me, Franklin Roosevelt, World War II, Harry Truman, John F. Kennedy, Lyndon Johnson, and Vietnam, all subjects I have written about, keep coming up; they echo Peter Gayle's comment that history is argument without end.

When Susan Ferber suggested that I condense my eight-hundred-page biography of John F. Kennedy to mark the fiftieth anniversary of his inauguration as president, it became an opportunity to revisit the many questions that had originally drawn me to Kennedy, the man and the president. Why, almost fifty years after his death, does someone who served as president for only a thousand days command the continuing high regard so many in the United States and around the world have for him? This is especially puzzling in that revelations about his private life—his hidden medical history and obsessive womanizing—have become common knowledge.

What can be said about his brief term, which principally focused on foreign policy issues—Cuba, the Soviet Union, Vietnam, and Latin America? And what of his limited domestic achievements on issues he considered of vital moment to his presidential aspirations—civil rights, Medicare, federal aid to education, a tax cut to spur a sluggish economy, and a war on poverty?

Kennedy seems to provide enduring lessons about the power of a charismatic personality in contemporary politics. He also reminds us of the limits of military action, as he demonstrated through his cautionary dealings during the Bay of Pigs operation and the missile crisis in Cuba. His attraction to Edward Gibbon's adage—"There is nothing more contrary to nature than the attempt to hold in obedience distant provinces"—is a cautionary tale for our time as we confront decisions on expanded commitments in Afghanistan.

In short, Kennedy remains a fascinating subject for scrutiny—not only because we continue to wrestle with the issues of his day but also because he has much to tell us about the difficulties we face almost a half century after he lived.

John Fitzgerald Kennedy was born on May 29, 1917, into a prominent Irish family in Boston. His grandfathers, Patrick Joseph Kennedy and John E. Fitzgerald, were both impressively successful men: P.J., as friends called him, was a leading figure in Boston's liquor trade and a well-off banker; and Fitzie or Honey Fitz, as Bostonians came to know him, was a natural politician who won elections to the Massachusetts state senate, three terms as a U.S. congressman, and then repeated service as Boston's mayor. Fitzie's political magic was captured in a verse of the day: "Honey Fitz can talk you blind / on any subject you can find / Fish and fishing, motor boats / Railroads, street cars, getting votes." His gift of gab was known as Fitzblarney.

The offspring of P.J. and Honey Fitz, Joseph Patrick Kennedy and Rose Elizabeth Fitzgerald, married in 1914 to form a perfect union of Boston's "cut-glass" Irish, or FIFs ("First Irish Families"). Twenty-four-year-old Rose, who had been a Boston debutante, and twenty-six-year old Joe, who had graduated from Harvard and established himself as the city's youngest bank president, looked forward to privileged lives as upper-middle-class Bostonians. But Joe's ambitions reached beyond his local moorings to project him on to the national scene. Speculation in stocks after World War I made Joe a millionaire and opened the way to his accumulation of additional millions in the movie industry and the liquor business after the end of Prohibition in 1933. His standing as one of America's wealthiest businessmen combined with financial contributions to the Democratic Party generally, and Franklin Roosevelt's election campaign specifically, to win Joe appointment as the first chairman of the Securities and Exchange Commission in 1934, in 1937 as chair of the U.S. Maritime Commission, and later that year as ambassador to Great Britain. Although Joe's identification with Neville Chamberlain's appeasement policies would bring an end to his personal political ambitions, his term as ambassador won his family a place in the *Social Register,* an achievement that gave him life-long satisfaction.

John Kennedy was the second of nine children born to Rose and Joe between 1915 and 1932. The first, Joe, Jr., was the son his father anointed to become America's first Irish Catholic president. But when he was killed in World War II in a mission to attack German buzz bombs launched from Belgian installations, Jack inherited his father's political ambitions.

Jack was initially an unlikely candidate for public office. Although he had served heroically in the war as a PT boat commander who had rescued his crew when a Japanese destroyer had cut his boat in half, Jack was more interested in writing about public affairs than managing them. His senior thesis at Harvard, published in 1940 as a book—*Why England Slept*—was a discussion of Britain's failure in the 1930s to heed Winston Churchill's warnings and meet the Nazi challenge. In 1945, after leaving the navy, Jack had worked as a newspaper correspondent covering the founding of the United Nations in San Francisco.

In 1946, however, backed by his father's money, he won election as a U.S. congressional representative from Boston. His three terms in the House were little more than a way station: after the excitement of the notoriety that had come to him from publishing a book and winning a medal in the war, his work in Congress bored him; he resented the arcane rules and customs that made it impossible for him as a junior member of the chamber to make some kind of big mark. "We were just worms in the House—nobody paid much attention to us nationally," he said.

In 1952, he ran for a Senate seat against the Massachusetts incumbent Henry Cabot Lodge, whose storied family background was captured in the saying "Up in Boston, where the Lodges speak only to Cabots and the Cabots speak only to God." As in 1946, Joe put his financial resources behind Jack's campaign and made Robert Kennedy, Jack's younger brother, the campaign's manager. As two journalists wrote, Bobby gave the campaign "organization, organization, and more organization." The result was "the most methodical, the most scientific, the most thoroughly detailed, the most intricate, the most disciplined and smoothly working state-wide campaign in Massachusetts history—and possibly anywhere else."

In the end, the election turned more on charisma than on issues or even the financial wherewithal or organizational brilliance that Joe and Bobby brought to the table. Two of Jack's aides believed that "Kennedy won on his personality—apparently he was the new kind of political figure that the people were looking for that year, dignified and gentlemanly and well-educated and intelligent, without the air of superior condescension that other cultured politicians, such as Lodge and Adlai Stevenson [the Democratic Party's 1952 presidential candidate], too often displayed before audiences." In a year when the Republicans, led by Dwight D. Eisenhower, their popular presidential candidate, won the White House and control of both congressional houses, Jack's victory was a testimony to his emerging political star power. The fact that only one other Democratic congressman, George Smathers of Florida, was able to win a Senate seat in 1952 gave Jack instant standing as a force in his party.

He found service in the Senate only a little more satisfying than service in the House. The constant demands of state interests meant spending time and energy wrestling with problems that diverted his attention from national security issues, his principal concern. It was the international perils of the 1950s that particularly attracted Jack's attention—ending the Korean War, the need to counter Soviet Russia's acquisition of atomic bombs, and the fight for hearts and minds in Third World countries across Asia and Africa that were being courted by Communist propaganda from Moscow and Peking, where the three-year-old Chinese Communist regime railed against U.S. imperialism.

Kennedy believed it was essential that he speak out on defense issues. In May 1953, he said that Moscow might continue to rely "on the weapons of subversion, economic disintegration and guerilla warfare to accomplish our destruction, rather than upon the direct assault of an all-out war. But we cannot count on it." He became a strong advocate of America's need "to build irresistible military strength." In taking up the cause of national security, Kennedy understood that he was aligning himself with a majority of Americans—56 percent of whom in April 1954 were primarily concerned about threats of war, Communist subversion, and national defense. Some critics complained that Kennedy's stance was essentially political posturing. Although it was shrewd politics, Kennedy denied that his motives were less than noble: He said that this was not an issue "on which the Democrats [or he] can win elections, for only disaster can prove us correct."

There is no question that Kennedy was already looking toward the day when he could run for president as a senator who had made his mark on national security questions. But it is also clear that he had a genuine interest in finding answers to international conflicts. In the first year of his term, he fixed attention on the French conflict in Indochina, where Communist insurgents were fighting to overturn French colonial rule. He openly urged the French to promise independence to Cambodia, Laos, and Vietnam and argued strongly against U.S. military intervention to help the French defeat a popular uprising. In a Senate speech, he declared, "No amount of American military assistance in

Indochina can conquer…'an enemy of the people' which has the sympathy and covert support of the people."

Winning appointment to the Senate Foreign Relations Committee in 1957, Kennedy had a platform for additional pronouncements on foreign affairs. In a Senate speech in July 1957, he declared that "the most powerful single force in the world today is neither communism nor capitalism, neither the H-Bomb nor the guided missile—it is man's eternal desire to be free and independent." And "the single most important test of American foreign policy today is how we meet the challenge of imperialism." Specifically, he was referring to anticolonialism and the rebellion against French rule in Algeria. He urged U.S. backing for Algerian self-determination through a mediated settlement. If the French refused to negotiate, he favored outright U.S. support of independence.

Because both the French and the Eisenhower White House opposed his initiative, Kennedy came to fear that his outspokenness had been a mistake that would cost him dearly in the run for president in 1960 that he and his father were planning. But Joe assured him otherwise: "You lucky mush," Joe said; "You don't know it and neither does anyone else, but within a few months everyone is going to know just how right you were on Algeria." Joe was right.

A larger obstacle stood in the way of a possible successful run for the White House—a number of health problems that had dogged him since childhood. From the time he was three, not a year passed without one physical affliction or another. Two months before his third birthday, scarlet fever compelled his hospitalization for two months, followed by two weeks in a Maine sanatorium. A variety of maladies forced him during his preteen years to spend a considerable amount of time in bed or at least indoors convalescing.

In 1934, at age thirteen, he suffered from an undiagnosed illness that caused him abdominal pains, weight loss, and fatigue. Continual bouts of intestinal troubles over the next four years landed him for a month in the Mayo Clinic in Rochester, Minnesota. He was diagnosed with spastic colitis, a chronic problem that he wished to keep secret. "What will I say when someone asks me what I got?" he wrote his closest friend at school. Jack and his family were determined to hide the seriousness of his medical problems. They believed that nothing good could come of revealing that Jack might have some debilitating long-term illnesses that could play havoc with his future.

In 1937, while a student at Harvard, he began relying on newly available steroids to control his colitis. Physicians in the 1930s and 1940s did not realize what is now common medical knowledge: steroids are effective in treating colitis but can have deleterious long-term chronic effects, including osteoporosis that deteriorates the spine and suppression of normal adrenal function. It is conceivable that in Jack's case, the onset of Addison's disease (a malfunction of the adrenal glands characterized by a deficiency of the hormones needed to regulate blood sugar, sodium, potassium, and the response to stress) and of severe pain of the lumbar spine were triggered by the steroids.

By the 1950s, Jack's back problems had become so severe that he could not pull a sock on his left foot and had to climb and descend stairs sideways. Despite the dangers of back surgery for someone with Addison's disease, Jack was determined to risk death rather than spend the rest of his life hobbled by pain. The surgery in October 1954 was a limited success, and a postoperative infection caused a priest to give him last rites. He did not recover until May 1955, and he remained vulnerable to a variety of illnesses: between May 1955 and October 1957, he was hospitalized nine times—a total of forty-four days, including two weeklong stays and one nineteen-day stretch.

The state of Jack's health was a closely guarded secret. Apparently, only his parents, his wife, Jacqueline, who had become vital to his political advancement since he had married her in 1953, his brother Bobby, and his doctors knew the full extent of his various maladies. His youngest brother, Edward (Ted) Kennedy, stated in a 2009 memoir that he never knew how many illnesses Jack had struggled with until his health records were revealed in 2002–3. Even Jack's various doctors, who were closed off from one another, did not know the full extent of his medical problems.

Although Jack never made much of a mark in the Senate, he believed that conditions in 1958–60, the last two years of Eisenhower's second term, gave a Democrat a good chance to win the White House. And Kennedy was convinced that his candidacy would offer an attractive alternative to recent Republican control of national and international affairs. A sluggish economy and racial tensions at home and Soviet advances abroad—especially the launching of *Sputnik,* a space satellite that signaled a Communist advantage over the United States in space exploration and intercontinental missile launchers—suggested that voters would be eager for a change in 1960.

Kennedy's greatest asset may have been his youth and his standing as a relative newcomer on the national scene. At age forty three he would be the youngest man voters ever elevated to the presidency. Only Theodore Roosevelt, who came to office in 1901 after William McKinley's assassination, had been younger. But Kennedy's youth also bespoke inexperience. In addition, as a Catholic, he had to convince voters that his religion formed no risk to the tradition of separation of church and state or, specifically, that the Church in Rome would in no way shape his decisions as president.

His initial challenge was to win primary contests against other Democratic contenders and convince his party's bosses that he could in fact win the White House. There could be no doubt that by 1960 he had become a popular public figure. In 1957 alone, he had more than twenty-five hundred speaking invitations around the country and agreed to give 144 talks, nearly one every other day, in forty-seven states. By 1960, a majority of the Democratic Party's state chairs described him as the likely choice, and 409 of the 1,220 delegates to the 1956 Democratic Convention, who expected to be delegates again, declared their intentions to support his nomination. Democratic governors predicted that while Jack might not win on the first ballot, he would certainly be the front runner. Yet no one was ready to anoint him: After a group of reporters met with him in 1958, they "looked at him walking out of the room, thin, slender, almost boyish," and one of them said, "'Can you imagine that young fellow thinking he could be President of the United States any time soon?"

Yet Kennedy did well in straw polls that matched him against his likely Republican opponent, Vice President

Richard M. Nixon, who had a commanding lead for his party's nomination. Yet no sitting vice president since Martin Van Buren in 1836 had won the White House. Moreover, the polls gave Kennedy the edge in a contest with Nixon. Still, Kennedy's margin of victory in these polls was small, and they gave no indication that he and the Democrats could take anything for granted.

To win the Democratic nomination, he first had to convince the party bosses and convention delegates that he could win primary elections against Senator Hubert Humphrey of Minnesota, his principal opponent, first in Wisconsin and then in West Virginia. Humphrey, an outspoken civil rights advocate, was the darling of the party's liberals, whose support was critical for any Democrat to win the nomination and the election. They saw Kennedy as an ambitious but superficial playboy with little more to recommend him than his good looks and charm: on none of the issues most important to them—McCarthyism, civil rights, and labor unions—had Jack been an outspoken advocate. They also distrusted his father, whom they saw as a robber baron and prewar appeaser of Nazi Germany. When someone asked former president Harry Truman if he was concerned about Jack Kennedy's ties to his conservative Catholic Church, Truman replied, "It's not the Pope I'm worried about, it's the pop." Eleanor Roosevelt, a leading party liberal—referring to Jack's 1956 book *Profiles in Courage* and his equivocation about Joe McCarthy—complained, "I wish young Kennedy would show less profile and more courage."

Wisconsin, Humphrey's next-door neighbor, with a large Protestant population, was a crucial test of Kennedy's voter appeal. Jack threw himself into the campaign as if defeat would signal the end of his presidential bid—as the Kennedys believed it would. At the end of his six-week campaign from mid-February to early April, Jack won a solid victory, with 56.5 percent of the vote, which entitled him to 60 percent of Wisconsin's convention delegates. But because so much of his vote had come from Catholic enclaves around the state, this victory did nothing to refute the skepticism about his ability to get Protestant votes. When one of his sisters asked what his success in Wisconsin meant, he replied, "It means we have to go to West Virginia and do it all over again."

West Virginia, with a 96 percent Protestant population, now became his essential proving ground. Spending two weeks on nonstop campaigning, he pressed the case for himself as a firm believer in FDR's New Deal, a patriot whose brother had died in the war and who had seen navy combat in the southwest Pacific, an American who put his country above his religion, and a potential president who would not forget the needs of West Virginians. He combined his personal appeal with extensive radio and television ads and generous payoffs to county Democratic leaders, who turned out enough voters to give him a landslide—60.8 to 39.2 percent. Although it required considerable hard work at the convention in Los Angeles, Jack, leaning on his brother Bobby's organizing skills, won the nomination on the first ballot.

Because the election threatened to be close, Jack reached out to Senator Lyndon B. Johnson of Texas (LBJ) as his running mate. With the normally solidly Democratic South likely to resist putting in the White House a Catholic from the Northeast Kennedy hoped that LBJ's presence on the ticket could improve the chances of winning Texas and other southern states. But would LBJ accept? As a rival for the nomination and a domineering personality who had been Senate majority leader and saw Jack as distinctly junior to himself, LBJ seemed unlikely to accept second chair. But LBJ, convinced that he would wield limited power in the Senate if Kennedy won the White House, accepted the vice presidential nomination in the hope that he could be a dominant force in a Kennedy administration.

Taking LBJ as vice president proved to be a master stroke. This presidential election was the closest one since Woodrow Wilson's victory in 1912. From the beginning, the polls showed that Nixon, the Republican candidate, was locked in a nip-and-tuck race with Kennedy. Having served eight years as Eisenhower's vice president, Nixon emphasized his superior executive experience, especially in foreign affairs, and claimed that he would be a more reliable defender of the nation's security in the Cold War than Kennedy with his youth and untested background. Kennedy pointed to the problems associated with the Eisenhower administration's watch, with which Nixon was so closely identified: economic recessions with stagnating growth, a racial divide between whites and blacks that threatened to test the country's social fabric, a "missile gap" that supposedly made the United States vulnerable to a Soviet nuclear attack, and Fidel Castro's pro-Soviet regime in Cuba that jeopardized U.S. interests in the Western Hemisphere.

Three key moments in the contest gave Kennedy an edge on Election Day. The first was a televised speech in September 1960 before a gathering of Protestant ministers in a Houston hotel ballroom, viewed by millions of Americans. Kennedy emphasized that he saw far more critical issues before the country—"war and hunger and ignorance and despair"—than his religion. Nevertheless, he felt compelled to assure his audience that he believed the separation of church and state was absolute and that his church would have no influence on his actions as president. His poise and restraint in the face of some hostile questions won the appreciation of his audience, which stood and applauded at the close of the meeting. His performance substantially muted concerns about his Catholicism.

Second, because so many liberals were disappointed with Kennedy's nomination over Humphrey and Stevenson, both of whom were more outspoken advocates of civil rights reforms, Kennedy needed to take some step during the campaign that solidified his standing among liberals generally and blacks in particular. The opportunity arose when Martin Luther King, head of the Southern Christian Leadership Conference and the country's most visible advocate of nonviolent resistance to racial segregation, was imprisoned in Georgia for trying to integrate an Atlanta restaurant and sentenced to a four-month term of hard labor for violating his probation on a minor, trumped-up traffic violation. In response, Jack called King's wife to express sympathy and offer help in any way he could. When Bobby Kennedy, Jack's campaign manager, successfully lobbied a Georgia judge to free King, it decisively tipped the black vote to Kennedy and gave him an edge in five closely contested swing states.

The third and most decisive development favoring Kennedy was a televised debate with Nixon on September 26 at a Chicago CBS studio. Some seventy million Americans, nearly two-thirds of the country's adult population, tuned in. Kennedy believed that if he just held his own, it would diminish Nixon's claims of superior preparation to hold the highest office.

Kennedy outdid Nixon in almost every way. Kennedy gained an initial advantage by addressing his opening statement directly to the American people. He did the same in his closing statement. By contrast, Nixon used his introduction and summary to draw contrasts between himself and Kennedy. The difference was telling: Kennedy came across as a leader who intended to deal with the nation's greatest problems; Nixon registered on voters as someone trying to gain an advantage over an adversary. Nixon impressed viewers as unstatesmanlike, confirming the negative impression many had of him from earlier campaigns and public actions that won him the unflattering nickname "Tricky Dick."

Kennedy also got the better of Nixon because he looked more relaxed, more in command of himself, or, as the journalist Theodore White noted in his chronicle of the campaign, "calm and nerveless.... The Vice-President, by contrast, was tense, almost frightened, at turns glowering and, occasionally, haggard-looking to the point of sickness." The camera showed Nixon "half-slouched, his 'Lazy Shave' powder faintly streaked with sweat, his eyes exaggerated hollows of blackness, his jaws, jowls, and face drooping with strain." Chicago's mayor Richard Daley said, "My God! They've embalmed him before he even died." In addition, against the light gray stage backdrop,

Nixon, dressed in a light gray suit, "faded into fuzzed outline, while Kennedy in his dark suit had the crisp picture edge of contrast." Not yet fully recovered from a recent hospitalization for an infected knee and exhausted by intense campaigning, Nixon appeared scrawny and listless.

Ironically, Kennedy, whose medical problems greatly exceeded anything Nixon had, appeared to be the picture of robust good health. Kennedy further seized the advantage during the debate when he looked bored or amused as Nixon spoke, as if he were thinking, "How silly." Yet those who heard the debate on the radio thought that Nixon had won—demonstrating the importance of the contrasting televised images and signaling the significant role television would play in future campaigns.

Yet Kennedy's debate victory hardly settled the outcome of the election. With the religious issue still a force in voter thinking and his youth continuing to pose concerns about his capacity to respond effectively to the Soviet threat, his final victory had a paper-thin margin. Out of 68,837,000 popular votes, he won by only 118,574 ballots, or 49.72 percent. (Senator Harry F. Byrd of Virginia, running as a segregationist, siphoned off some five hundred thousand votes.) Kennedy's margin in the electoral column was a more robust 303 to 219, but the election wasn't settled until noon of the next day when Nixon conceded.

In the final analysis, a number of things explain Kenney's victory: a faltering economy in an election year; anxiety about the nation's apparently diminished ability to meet the Soviet threat; Kennedy's decidedly greater personal charm alongside Nixon's abrasiveness before the television cameras and on the stump; LBJ's help in winning seven southern states; an effective get-out-the-vote campaign among Democrats, who, despite Eisenhower's two elections, remained the majority party; the black vote for Kennedy; and the backing of ethnic voters, including but much broader than Catholics, in big cities.

With the election in hand, Kennedy turned in the ten weeks before his inauguration to the challenge of selecting a cabinet. Because his margin of victory had been so small, he was concerned to make his administration as bipartisan as possible, especially on foreign policy and national security issues, where the Republicans had described the Democrats as too weak in responding to the Communist threat. Kennedy was intent on conciliating Republicans by choosing a secretary of the treasury, secretary of defense, and national security adviser from their ranks and demonstrating that he intended to put the national interest above partisan politics.

Before he chose any of these officials, he announced that he would keep on Eisenhower's appointees, Allen Dulles and J. Edgar Hoover, as heads of the CIA and the FBI, respectively. Kennedy hoped this would put Democrats on notice that he would not be beholden to any party faction and would make up his own mind about what would best serve the country and his administration. (He may also have been guarding against damaging leaks from Hoover about his private life and his history of womanizing. As LBJ famously put it later when he continued Hoover's service in office, it was better to keep Hoover inside the tent pissing out than outside the tent pissing in.)

For Treasury, Kennedy selected C. Douglas Dillon, an imposing establishment figure and a pillar of the New York banking community. A former ambassador to France, undersecretary of state for economic affairs, and undersecretary in the Eisenhower administration, Dillon was a liberal Republican who put national needs above party loyalty.

For state, Kennedy chose Dean Rusk, the president of the Rockefeller Foundation, who had served as assistant secretary of state for the Far East under Truman. Rusk seemed certain to be a faceless, faithful bureaucrat who would serve rather than attempt to lead. Determined to run foreign policy from the White House, Kennedy saw Rusk as the perfect man for the job. Although Rusk was something of a Cold War liberal hawk, his reputation for discretion made it more than likely that he would be the kind of passive administrator Kennedy wanted running the State Department. Kennedy would not be disappointed: he soon joked about Rusk's caution and affinity for a low profile by telling friends that when he and Rusk were alone, Rusk would whisper that there were still too many others present.

For defense, Kennedy decided on Robert S. McNamara, president of the Ford Motor Company. Appreciating that any misstep on defense policy would become a political liability, Kennedy was determined to select someone who would have immediate standing as an aggressive defender of the national security. McNamara was a nominal Republican with impeccable credentials as a businessman and service as an air force officer during World War II, when he had increased the effectiveness of the nation's air power by applying a system of statistical control. He was universally recognized for being exceptionally intelligent, tough-minded, independent, and a managerial whiz with the skills to make the unwieldy Defense Department more effective in serving the national security.

McNamara initially resisted the appointment, telling Kennedy that he was not qualified to serve in the job. Kennedy countered with the assertion that there was no school for defense secretaries or presidents. After Kennedy had pressured McNamara to take the post by leaking news of his appointment to the press and McNamara had spoken to departing defense secretary Thomas Gates, he told Kennedy that he believed he could handle the job. Kennedy teased: "I talked over the presidency with Eisenhower, and after hearing what it's all about, I'm convinced I can handle it."

Kennedy's most controversial selection was the appointment of his brother Bobby as attorney general. Jack confided to former secretary of state Dean Acheson that he had little acquaintance with the members of his cabinet and said he "felt he had to have someone whom he knew very well and trusted completely with whom he could just sort of put his feet up and talk things over." Besides, the attorney general's job was certain to be at the center of the civil rights controversies that were bound to crop up in the next four years, and he wanted someone in the office he could depend on to not only adjudicate disputes but also defend him against political attacks. He also believed that Bobby would be invaluable as someone who would tell him "the unvarnished truth, no matter what."

The appointment stirred controversy as an act of nepotism. Jack tried to blunt the complaints by joking that he just wanted to give Bobby, who had a law degree from the University of Virginia, "a little legal practice before he becomes a lawyer." Jack told his friend Ben Bradlee, editor of *Newsweek,* that he would like to open the front door of his house at about two o'clock in the morning, to look up and down the street, and if no one was there, to whisper "It's Bobby." To divert criticism from himself, Jack put out the story that his father had insisted on rewarding Bobby for his management of the campaign with the cabinet post. Although LBJ shared the view that it was "a disgrace for a kid who's never practiced law to be appointed," he played the good soldier and carried out Jack's instructions to talk senators into approving Bobby's appointment.

Kennedy believed that what he said and the impression he made on the country at the start of his term were vital to building an image of a new administration more vigorously engaged by national and international problems than its predecessor. He saw no single element as more important in launching his presidency than a compelling inaugural address. He considered it an opportunity to inspire renewed national confidence and hope. His speech, which at 1,355 words was a model of succinctness, especially compared with the previous forty-four inaugurals, which averaged 2,599 words, impressed commentators then and after as one of the great inaugurals of American history.

The speech, like Thomas Jefferson's inaugural in 1801, began by emphasizing not partisanship but shared national values: "We are all Federalists. We are all Republicans,"

Jefferson said. Kennedy declared: "We observe today not a victory of party but a celebration of freedom.... Let every nation know, whether it wishes us well or ill, that we shall pay any price, bear any burden, meet any hardship, support any friend, oppose any foe to assure the survival and success of liberty." This would include "a new alliance for progress" with the nation's neighbors to the south.

Focused almost exclusively on foreign challenges, the speech was a call to national commitment and sacrifice. "Now the trumpet summons us again—not as a call to battle, though embattled we are—but a call to bear the burden of a long twilight struggle...a struggle against the common enemies of man: tyranny, poverty, disease and war itself.... And so, my fellow Americans: ask not what your country can do for you—ask what you can do for your country."

To give substance to his remarks, in the first days of his presidency, Kennedy established the Peace Corps, enlisting young Americans "to help foreign countries meet their urgent needs for skilled manpower." The Corps was not to be "an instrument of diplomacy or propaganda or ideological conflict." Instead, it would allow "our people to exercise more fully their responsibilities in the great common cause of world development." At the same time, Kennedy encouraged America's southern neighbors to believe that his Alliance for Progress—an alliance between the United States and Latin America to advance economic development, democratic institutions, and social justice—would promote social change in the hemisphere.

Although Kennedy launched the Alliance in a White House speech before congressional leaders and hemisphere ambassadors that excited hopes of dramatic change for the better, there were understandable doubts. One speech, however sincerely delivered, was not enough to convince his audience that traditional neglect of the region was at an end. Latin American representatives to the United States could not shun the belief that Kennedy's idealism was little more than a tool for combating Communism. Some derisively called the Alliance for Progress the Fidel Castro Plan.

Doubts about Kennedy's intentions toward Latin America intensified with the failure of an invasion by Cuban exiles of Cuba—at the Bay of Pigs—that was financed, trained, and equipped by the United States.

During 1959–60, as Castro, who had overturned the corrupt regime of Fulgencio Batista, denounced the United States as an imperialist opponent of progressive governments throughout the world and identified himself with the Communist governments in Moscow and Peking, the Eisenhower administration had planned Castro's ouster with an invasion by Cuban exiles. Warned from the start of his term that Castro aimed to facilitate Communist revolutions in Latin America, Kennedy was encouraged to endorse the Eisenhower plan for ridding Cuba and the hemisphere of Castro and his government.

Conflicting opinions from national security officials on the likely results of an invasion raised doubts for Kennedy as to the wisdom of an invasion. Where the military and the CIA predicted that it would touch off a full-scale civil war that would bring down Castro, the State Department worried that it would produce "very grave" political consequences in the United Nations and Latin America, where the Alliance for Progress would be seen as nothing more than public relations.

Kennedy faced two unhappy choices. If he decided against an invasion, he would risk public attacks on him from the exiles and the right wing in the United States for failing to combat Communism in the hemisphere. He would be called an appeaser of Castro and another Democratic president afraid to roll back a Communist advance. If he approved an invasion, he risked touching off an international disaster: protests against U.S. imperialism seemed certain to erupt around the world and especially in Third world countries that he was eager to woo away from Communist enticements.

When the military and CIA assured him that an invasion could succeed without direct U.S. military action in support of the exiles, he agreed to go ahead, but on the condition that there be no overt American military involvement. The assurances to him included qualifiers that even if the invasion did not immediately topple Castro, the invaders would be able to take refuge in the surrounding mountains, from where they could continue the insurgency until Castro fell. In assuring Kennedy that the invasion would eventually succeed, the CIA and military did not acknowledge that if the invasion forces became bogged down, the United States would have no choice but to intervene.

Last-minute warnings against an attack from Acheson and Senate Foreign Relations Committee chairman J. William Fulbright did not convince Kennedy to call a halt. When Kennedy told Acheson that Castro could put twenty-five thousand men on the beaches to oppose the fifteen hundred invaders, Acheson replied, "It doesn't take Price-Waterhouse to figure out that fifteen hundred aren't as good as twenty-five thousand." Fulbright rejected the need for action against a government that was more a thorn in the flesh than a dagger in the heart. Fearing the potential political heat if he stopped the invasion and succumbing to CIA and military assurances of success, Kennedy allowed the operation to go forward on April 17, three months into his term.

It was a miserable failure, with over one hundred invaders killed and another twelve hundred captured and imprisoned. The defeat was a terrible blow to a president who had been so intent on raising American spirits and convincing the world that his administration meant a turn toward greater international harmony. "How could I have been so stupid?" Kennedy openly asked himself in the aftermath of the defeat. Sobered by the setback and feeling guilty about the men who had died on the beaches and those who were now being held in Castro's prisons, Kennedy described the setback as "the worst experience of my life." He bravely accepted responsibility for the failure, quoting "an old saying that victory has a hundred fathers and defeat is an orphan." He told the press: "I'm the responsible officer of the Government."

Kennedy believed that overseas perils should take priority over economic and social reforms. As he told Nixon after the Bay of Pigs debacle, "It really is true that foreign affairs are the only important issue for a President to handle.... I mean, who gives a shit if the minimum wage is $1.15 or $1.25, in comparison to something like this."

Yet Kennedy also believed that an effective foreign policy partly depended on a strong economy and social cohesion at home. But his frustration with persuading Congress to act on a bold program of reforms was as great as his initial disappointment with making a gain abroad.

His first two initiatives—a cabinet department of urban affairs and housing to halt the deterioration of the country's urban areas and a tax cut to spur the economy—could not overcome the resistance of southern Democrats in Congress, who saw the proposed cabinet post as mainly serving inner-city blacks, and business leaders, who saw Kennedy's tax reform as at odds with their interests.

The failure of these two proposals signaled the hurdles Kennedy faced in trying to win passage of a broader set of tax reductions; federal aid to elementary, secondary, and higher education; health insurance for the elderly; and a civil rights bill to meet demands for equal treatment under the law for African-Americans suffering racial segregation and bars to voting in the form of poll taxes and literacy tests.

The opposition from southerners in Congress to civil rights legislation was so overt and likely to sidetrack efforts to win approval for the administration's other reforms that Kennedy didn't even bother to put a bill before the legislators. Opinion surveys bolstered Kennedy's timidity on civil rights. Although two-thirds of the populace said they favored desegregation of public schools as mandated by the Supreme Court in its famous 1954 *Brown v. Board of Education* decision, 68 percent of Americans backed giving public money to segregated schools if Kennedy's federal aid to education bill passed. Moreover, 61 percent of Americans supported gradual, as opposed to immediate, integration of the races in public places of accommodation. Only 24 percent of the country sympathized with the Freedom Riders, who were risking their lives by trying to integrate buses traveling across state lines in the South.

In 1961, none of Kennedy's reform proposals emerged from congressional committees. Federal involvement in education was anathema to conservatives, who wished to preserve local control. Emotional arguments about public funding for parochial schools opened an unbridgeable gap between Catholics and Protestants. Determined to keep his campaign pledges on separation of church and state, Kennedy provoked unyielding opposition from Catholics for refusing to support direct aid to parochial schools. While some critics of his stand on education protested his adherence to traditional thinking, his advocacy of health insurance for the elderly provoked the opposite response: warnings against administration plans to imitate communist countries by socializing medicine.

While Kennedy more or less passively accepted the congressional impasse over his domestic proposals, he was determined to fix the country's attention on the need for foreign policy gains. At the end of May, after a trip to Canada in which he pressed the prime minister to join the Organization of American States as a demonstration of hemispheric solidarity against Communist aggression, Kennedy spoke at a joint session of Congress in an effort to restore confidence in his foreign policy leadership.

Specifically, he asked Congress to fund an all-out effort to land a man on the Moon by the end of the decade. Such a mission, he believed, would be of compelling value in the contest with the Soviets for international prestige, as well as a way to convince allies and neutral Third World nations of America's technical superiority to Moscow. Because a majority of Americans—58 percent—thought that *Sputnik* demonstrated that the Soviets might get to the Moon first, they opposed spending an estimated $40 billion on a space race. But Kennedy refused to accept a timid approach to space exploration. He was convinced that it would not only yield technological, economic, and political advantages but also boost America's world image. "We choose to go to the moon in this decade," he said, "and do other things, not because they are easy, but because they are hard; because that goal will serve to organize and measure the best of our energies and skills."

Kennedy's speech was also a forum for justifying a trip to Europe to meet with French president Charles de Gaulle in Paris and Soviet first secretary Nikita Khrushchev in Vienna. De Gaulle's leadership in reestablishing France as an important power after her defeat in World War II had made him one of the storied figures of the century;

Kennedy called him "a great captain of the Western World." Kennedy saw a meeting with him as a chance to establish himself as an American president in a league with an international icon. Although Kennedy understood that differences with de Gaulle over various issues—nuclear weapons (France wanted her own arsenal), NATO, which de Gaulle saw as an alliance Washington controlled for its own purposes, and Southeast Asia, which de Gaulle believed should be more peripheral to Western security than Washington did—would not be resolved by his visit, he assumed that de Gaulle would encourage a public view of Franco-American harmony and of two presidents meeting as equals.

Kennedy was not disappointed. When de Gaulle told him that intervention in Southeast Asia would be "a bottomless military and political quagmire," Kennedy expressed the hope: "You will not say that in public." De Gaulle replied, "Of course not. I never speak to the press. Never." So the conference was a case study in symbols over substance. Photographs and television images of the two standing together were by themselves a boost to Kennedy's prestige. The legendary de Gaulle treating Kennedy as an equal immediately raised him to the level of world statesman. His was an image of vibrancy, competence, and strength. At the end of his Paris visit, a column in the *International Herald Tribune* reflected a renewed confidence in Kennedy's leadership: The president, the columnist explained, "intends to act not only as his own foreign minister but as his own Soviet expert, French expert, Berlin expert, Laotian expert, nuclear test ban expert, etc."

An unexpected boost to Kennedy's standing came from the public impressions Jacqueline Kennedy made. Her command of the French language and expressions of regard for French culture and taste made her an instant hit with the French, who lined up by the thousands to catch a glimpse of her passing automobile or arrivals at and departures from well-publicized ceremonies. Dazzled by her knowledge of French history and art, de Gaulle publicly spoke of Jackie's "charm." The French press, thrilled by her appearance in a white silk Givenchy gown, anointed her "a queen" and described the Kennedy–de Gaulle dinner as an "Apotheosis at Versailles." Kennedy delighted French and American journalists with his opening remarks at a Paris press luncheon: "I do not think it altogether inappropriate to introduce myself to this audience. I am the man who accompanied Jacqueline Kennedy to Paris, and I have enjoyed it."

The principal point of the trip was to meet Khrushchev and especially talk to him about Germany and Berlin. A reunified and rearmed Germany that could inflict a new round of havoc on the Soviet Union like that of World

War II was Moscow's constant fear. Consequently, a separate East German state had been central to its German policy throughout the fifties. By 1961, the embarrassing exodus of East Germans and other Eastern Europeans to the West through Berlin provoked the Soviets into warnings that they would sign a peace treaty with East Germany. They believed that this would create an independent state that could then choose to end Allied rights in three of Berlin's four occupation zones by integrating the city, which was located 110 miles from the West German border inside East Germany. Such a treaty promised to prevent the reunification of Germany, which Moscow so greatly feared would pose renewed threats to the Soviet Union.

Kennedy had two broad aims in coming to Vienna: a meeting with Khrushchev that could be described as a success would help repair the damage from the Bay of Pigs fiasco and could reduce the possibility of misunderstandings that might provoke a nuclear war. De Gaulle and leading U.S. experts on Soviet Russia assured Kennedy that Khrushchev did not want a war and in fact would like to see an improvement in U.S.-Soviet relations, as tensions had escalated over the shooting down of a U.S. spy plane scanning Soviet missile installations. George Kennan, the architect of America's so-called containment strategy for dealing with the Soviet Union, warned Kennedy that the Soviets might be intent on shattering

America's "world position and influence" by "an all-out propaganda attack that could include an effort to eclipse and embarrass the president at their summit talks."

Kennan had it right. At the first session of the summit on June 3, Khrushchev turned what Kennedy had hoped might be a discussion of current issues into a philosophical debate about the virtues of their respective systems. Khrushchev attacked the United States for aiming to liquidate Communism and declared that good relations between East and West depended on a mutual acceptance of each other's systems. Kennedy responded that it was not the United States but the Soviet Union that was unsettling the world, with its aggressive efforts to impose Communism on other countries. Khrushchev declared that Communism would win the East-West contest because history was on its side.

Kennedy tried to move the discussion back to current realities by urging a focus on means of averting conflict in areas where the two sides had clashing interests. But Khrushchev wouldn't let go of the larger point: that this was a contest of ideas that Communism would win. Kennedy emphasized the need to avoid a military confrontation. But Khrushchev demanded to know if Kennedy was saying that any expansion of Soviet influence would be seen as an excuse for a Soviet-American conflict. Before Kennedy could answer, Khrushchev dismissed the president's view that the spread of communist ideology would threaten the peace. Kennedy warned against miscalculations that could lead to war. Khrushchev contemptuously dismissed the talk of "miscalculation" as an excuse for getting the "USSR to sit like a schoolboy with his hands on his desk." Khrushchev called the talk of "miscalculation" a means to intimidate the Soviet Union.

Tensions eased a bit at lunch, when Kennedy asked about two medals on Khrushchev's jacket. He replied that they were Lenin Peace Prizes. Kennedy joked, "I hope you get to keep them." When Khrushchev joined in the laughter, Kennedy's press secretary had an anecdote he could share with the media that demonstrated Kennedy's quick wit and diplomatic skill.

But the levity was no more than a respite from Khrushchev's relentless verbal assaults. During a stroll in a garden after lunch, two of Kennedy's aides watched from an upstairs window while "Khrushchev was carrying on a heated argument, circling around Kennedy and snapping at him like a terrier and shaking his finger." Kennedy later described the first secretary as trying to score points at every turn. When Kennedy complained that the American government system imposed on him a "time-consuming process," Khrushchev shot back: "Well why don't you switch to our system?"

The afternoon's formal conversations produced more sparring and antagonism. When Kennedy explained that he had made a mistake in unleashing the invasion of Cuba, Khrushchev took it not as a conciliatory expression but another chance to denounce the United States as an imperialist power eager to repress the aspirations of the people and threaten Moscow with war when it objected to U.S. imperialism. Russia, by contrast, only wanted to keep the peace. After the afternoon meetings, Khrushchev described Kennedy to his comrades as "very young...not strong enough. Too intelligent and too weak." Khrushchev believed that if he bested Kennedy at the Vienna summit, it would undermine the United States' political standing. He had not come to negotiate. He had come to compete.

Kennedy was greatly troubled by the day's exchanges, especially Khrushchev's warnings that he would sign a peace treaty with Germany regardless of what the United States did. Kennedy complained to aides that Khrushchev "treated me like a little boy." The U.S. ambassador to Moscow tried to comfort the president by telling him that Khrushchev's behavior was "par for the course." Charles Bohlen, another Soviet expert, feared that Kennedy had gotten "a little bit out of his depth" by being drawn into an ideological debate. Kennan thought that Khrushchev had tied the president in knots and that Kennedy had appeared hesitant and overwhelmed. Yet it was absurd for Khrushchev to believe that scoring points against his younger opponent would do anything but stiffen Kennedy's resolve to meet the communist challenge. Khrushchev may have believed his own rhetoric and felt compelled to respond to pressure from comrades in the Kremlin and Chinese efforts to supplant Moscow as the leader of international Communism; but his bullying tactics were miserably shortsighted and raised the temperature of international hostilities.

At the second day of the summit, when Khrushchev began his hectoring again, Kennedy reprimanded him: "Look, Mr. Chairman," he said, "you aren't going to make a communist out of me and I don't expect to make a capitalist out of you. So let's get down to business."

But Khrushchev was not receptive to reaching agreements on a nuclear test ban agreement or Berlin, the two topics Kennedy raised with him during the second day's meetings. Reluctant to halt nuclear tests before reaching parity with the United States, Khrushchev insisted that general disarmament should precede a test ban. An exasperated Kennedy declared that "the conversation was back where it had started."

The discussion of Berlin was even more frustrating to Kennedy. Khrushchev's goals were to ensure that a reunited

Germany would be incapable of inflicting fresh suffering on Russia and that Berlin would not remain an escape hatch for those oppressed by Communism. Kennedy warned Khrushchev that the United States would not allow Moscow to force the Western allies out of Berlin. "We are in Berlin," he said, "not because of someone's sufferance. We fought our way there.... If we were expelled from that area and accepted the loss of our rights no one would have any confidence in the U.S. commitments and pledges." Khrushchev promised to act on a treaty by December, and Kennedy warned him against trying to unsettle the European balance as an act that could lead to war.

Kennedy asked Khrushchev to have a final meeting with him about the issues dividing them. "I can't leave here without giving it one more try," he said to an aide. But the final talks were no more constructive than the earlier ones. Each warned the other that their policies toward Berlin could lead to war. Khrushchev told Kennedy that it was the United States that was threatening to impose the calamity of war on the world, not the Soviet Union. "It is up to the U.S. to decide whether there will be war or peace," he said. Kennedy somberly answered, "Then, Mr. Chairman, there will be war. It will be a cold winter."

Kennedy could not hide his distress over the harsh exchanges, which promised worse relations. Before cameras, as the two men left the Soviet embassy, Khrushchev put on a show of merriment, but Kennedy was grim, unsmiling. In a conversation with *New York Times* columnist James Reston at the U.S. embassy, Kennedy came across as "very gloomy," describing the meetings as the "roughest thing in my life." He said that Khrushchev had "just beat [the] hell out of me" because of his weak showing at the Bay of Pigs. He felt that he now needed to convince Khrushchev that he could not be pushed around. He was angry at himself for having approved the Bay of Pigs operation and thinking that he could reduce differences with Khrushchev by rational explanation. He feared that his performance at the meeting had increased rather than diminished the chances of an East-West war.

Somehow, Kennedy could not believe that Khrushchev really meant to go to war over Berlin. He said, "It would be crazy, and I'm sure he's not crazy." He thought it would be "particularly stupid" for the Russians to fight a war that would destroy them for the sake of something less than their survival. Yet he understood that smaller issues than those at stake over Berlin had sparked past wars, including World War I. As he traveled home from Vienna, he believed that the greatest challenges to him as president now lay ahead.

Fortunately for the world, Khrushchev and the Soviets were not mad: In mid-August, Moscow solved its Berlin refugee problem by erecting a wall between the city's eastern and western zones. The Berlin Wall, as the thirteen-foot barrier came to be known, was something of a godsend. "Why should Khrushchev put up a wall if he really intended to seize West Berlin?" Kennedy asked. "There wouldn't be any need of a wall if he occupied the whole city. This is his way out of his predicament. It's not a very nice solution, but a wall is a hell of a lot better than a war." Because he had no intention of posing a military challenge to Khrushchev's action, Kennedy raised German morale by announcing an increase in the U.S. troop garrison in the city and sent LBJ and General Lucius D. Clay, the architect of the 1948 Berlin airlift that had saved the Western sector from a Soviet blockade, to Berlin to show the flag. Relieved of his émigré problem and as determined as Kennedy to avoid a nuclear war, Khrushchev announced his satisfaction with indications of Western interest in a solution to the German and West Berlin problems and the diminished need to sign a peace treaty that threatened to force an East-West confrontation over Western occupation troops in Berlin.

Kennedy had no illusion that reduced tensions over Germany promised a grand rapprochement in East-West relations or an easing of the Soviet-American contest for global influence. Russia might not force America out of Berlin or into the permanent partition of Germany, but if Russia established Communist governments across Latin America, Africa, and Asia, it would leave the United States and its allies surrounded by hostile regimes.

Kennedy was especially worried about the dangers of Communist advances in the Western Hemisphere if Castro were not checked. The Alliance for Progress was clearly no immediate or even long-term answer to hemispheric problems. Instead, Kennedy felt compelled to rely on covert operations to counter Castro and promote anticommunism across Latin America. As the Berlin and German problems diminished, Kennedy concluded that the Soviet-American struggle would shift to the Third World. Specifically, he hoped to find some way to remove Castro from power.

Kennedy now signed on to Operation Mongoose, which Bobby Kennedy was asked to oversee. Bobby described the program as aiming to "stir things up on the island with espionage, sabotage, general disorder, run & operated by Cubans themselves." The CIA took the operation as an invitation to proceed with schemes to assassinate Castro. Whether the president ever signed on to CIA assassination plots is unclear. He apparently feared that killing Castro might do more to strengthen his revolution in Cuba than undermine it. Nevertheless, there is evidence that the CIA was actively engaged in such discussions between 1960 and 1965. During the first half of 1962, Bobby Kennedy called ending Castro's regime "the top priority in the United States Government—all else is secondary."

Despite determined efforts to keep anti-Castro plots a secret, Khrushchev rightly suspected Kennedy's determination to bring down Cuba's pro-Soviet government. Seizing on Cuban eagerness for a defense against U.S. intervention in the island, Castro welcomed a Khrushchev plan to turn Cuba into a Soviet missile base. In May and June 1962, Khrushchev and Soviet military and political chiefs agreed to deploy on the island twenty-four medium-range missiles, which could travel 1,050 miles, and sixteen intermediate missiles, with a range of 2,100 miles. This would double the number of Soviet missiles that could reach the continental United States and significantly increase Moscow's balance of military power in its competition with Washington.

Khrushchev saw multiple benefits from the deployment of the Soviet missiles. It would deter an attack on Cuba, reduce China's growing influence in the island, keeping Cuba in the Soviet orbit, and give Moscow greater leverage in bargaining with Washington over Berlin. Specifically, it would provide a counter to America's deployment of seventeen Jupiter missiles in Turkey aimed at the Soviet Union. Khrushchev saw his Cuban initiative as giving the

Americans "back some of their own medicine." Although Khrushchev believed that Kennedy "would not set off a thermonuclear war if there were our warheads there," he was taking what Kennedy later called "one hell of a gamble."

On October 16, 1962, after much speculation by administration critics and press accounts that the Soviets were installing offensive missiles in Cuba, Kennedy received confirmation from U-2 reconnaissance photos that this was the case. None of the earlier Cold War confrontations—the Berlin blockade, the collapse of Chiang Kai-shek's Nationalist government, the Korean War, the Hungarian revolution of 1956, the Bay of Pigs—measured up to the dangers that now faced the Kennedy White House. Kennedy at once set up an executive committee of thirteen military and civilian national security officials to consider a response.

Kennedy's principal challenge was to remove the missiles without provoking a full-scale war. The option of a surprise air strike that was favored by Kennedy's military chiefs to eliminate the missile sites gave the president pause. He believed repeated bombings would be required to do the job and it would be condemned as a reminder of the Japanese attack on Pearl Harbor. Ambassador to the UN Adlai Stevenson warned that an air raid would provoke Soviet reprisals in Turkey and Berlin and would "risk starting a nuclear war." The Joint Chiefs urged a full-scale invasion of Cuba. But Kennedy resisted this advice, too. Bobby Kennedy, undoubtedly reflecting his brother's opinion, said, "We've fought for fifteen years with Russia to prevent a first strike against us. Now...we do that to a small country. I think it is a hell of a burden to carry."

Kennedy's preference was for a blockade and negotiations that could persuade Khrushchev to remove the missiles from Cuba. Kennedy and his civilian advisers agreed that they could always bomb the installations and invade Cuba should the diplomatic initiative fail. But the military chiefs were opposed to trying a blockade and negotiations. Maxwell Taylor, chairman of the Joint Chiefs, predicted that a failure to take military action would undermine America's international credibility. "If we don't respond here in Cuba," he said, "we think the credibility is sacrificed."

Air force chief Curtis LeMay was even more emphatic about immediate military steps. "This blockade and political action," he predicted, "I see leading into war. I don't see any other solution....This is almost as bad as the appeasement at Munich." LeMay indirectly threatened Kennedy with making his dissent public. "I think that a blockade and political talk, would be considered by a lot of our friends and neutrals as being a pretty weak response to this. And I'm sure a lot of our own citizens would feel that way, too. In other words, you're in a pretty bad fix at the present time."

LeMay's response angered Kennedy, who asked, "What did you say?" LeMay repeated himself: "You're in a pretty bad fix." Kennedy responded with a hollow laugh, "You're in there with me." After the meeting, Kennedy asked his aide Kenneth O'Donnell, "Can you imagine LeMay saying a thing like that? These brass hats have one great advantage in their favor. If we listen to them, and do what they want us to do, none of us will be alive later to tell them that they were wrong."

The Joint Chiefs were also angry. They thought Kennedy was making a mistake. They saw him as trying to do "the goddamn thing piecemeal." His approach was preventing them from doing their job. But army chief of staff Earle Wheeler advised that Kennedy was obviously set against military moves: "The political action of a blockade is really what he's [after]." And this despite the fact that several of the president's civilian advisers had concluded that an air strike was the best option. But when Bobby Kennedy asserted that the president saw a "sneak" air attack as a kind of Pearl Harbor that would kill thousands of Cubans and a lot of Russians and preferred a blockade that would "allow the Soviets some room for maneuver to pull back from their overextended position in Cuba," the issue was settled. The only revision was in

Kennedy's decision to call the blockade a "quarantine," which could more readily be described as less than an act of war and seemed less likely to draw comparisons to the Soviets' 1948 Berlin blockade.

As Kennedy prepared to speak to the nation about the crisis and inform Khrushchev of the blockade and propose discussions, he told Humphrey, "If I'd known the job was this tough, I wouldn't have beaten you in West Virginia." Humphrey answered, "I knew, and that's why I let you beat me." Facing the possibility of an imminent nuclear war, the pressure on Kennedy was unimaginable.

Kennedy sent Khrushchev a letter pressing him to work out their differences. He said, "I have not assumed that you or any other sane man would, in this nuclear age, plunge the world into war which it is crystal clear no country could win and which could only result in catastrophic consequences to the whole world, including the aggressor." He insisted that Khrushchev remove the missile bases and other offensive weapons in Cuba that were threatening Western Hemisphere nations. Kennedy's speech to the nation and the world left no doubt that the United States would not tolerate this threat to its security. A Soviet failure to stop its buildup would justify additional U.S. action beyond the "quarantine." He demanded prompt dismantling and withdrawal of all offensive weapons in Cuba under UN supervision. Any use of the weapons in Cuba would bring retaliation against the Soviet Union.

However eager Khrushchev was to face down the Americans, his understanding that an unbending posture would bring catastrophe to his people persuaded him to back off. He ordered Soviet ships proceeding toward Cuba to halt and turn around, and he agreed to remove the missiles from Cuba if the United States would pledge not to invade the island. As an afterthought, he demanded that the United States also remove its Jupiter missiles from Turkey in return for the Soviet Union dismantling its missiles. Kennedy agreed to a public pledge not to invade Cuba but insisted that the Jupiter swap, which he was willing to accept, not be part of the public exchange and only occur after the Cuban crisis ended. Khrushchev's retreat was an enormous relief to Kennedy. He told an aide, "An invasion would have been a mistake—a wrong use of our power. But the military are mad. They wanted to do this."

Kennedy was not only thankful that the crisis had ended but hoped that its resolution "might well open the door to the solution of other outstanding problems." In particular, he hoped that he and Khrushchev might find agreement on banning nuclear tests in the atmosphere or limiting the development of nuclear bombs to underground tests that could no longer pollute the environment. But it wasn't just a commitment to reducing contaminants in the world's air that drew Kennedy to a test ban; it was also a measure to inhibit the proliferation of nuclear weapons. His advisers told him that continued U.S. and Soviet testing would make it cheaper and easier to produce bombs. "The diffusion of nuclear technology...does seep out." In twenty-five years, "in the absence of a test ban, the risk of diffusion would be very great indeed."

Khrushchev saw reason to join in a ban. The escalating arms race was a heavy financial burden on the Soviet Union, and Khrushchev hoped that a test ban could be a prelude to blocking the Chinese, who were increasingly at odds with Moscow, from building bombs. In November 1962, after the Missile Crisis, Khrushchev told Kennedy that "conditions are emerging now for reaching an agreement on the prohibition of nuclear weapons [and the] cessation of all types of nuclear weapons tests."

Suspicions and doubts, however, stood in the way. Washington insisted on on-site inspections that Moscow resisted as likely to reveal its relatively weak nuclear capacity to the United States. The Soviets also worried that an agreement would open them to Chinese attacks for having signed a treaty that "betrayed" a Communist colleague. The Soviets were also motivated by an eagerness to buy time for additional nuclear tests that could make Soviet nuclear forces more competitive with those of the United States. On the American side, Senate opposition, fueled by warnings from the hawkish Joint Chiefs against anything but an airtight agreement with Moscow on verification, made it impossible for Kennedy to accept Soviet proposals that could be seen as giving them even the smallest leeway to cheat.

When discussions in the first four months of 1963 between U.S. and Soviet negotiators yielded little progress, Kennedy told a news conference that he would not give up on the talks. "Now, the reason why we keep moving and working on this question...is because personally I am haunted by the feeling that by 1970, unless we are successful, there may be ten nuclear powers instead of four, and by 1975, fifteen or twenty....I regard that as the greatest possible danger and hazard."

Kennedy decided to give negotiations a push with a "peace speech" on June 10, 1963, at the American University commencement. The speech was one of the great presidential statements of the twentieth century. Kennedy described his topic as the "most important...on Earth: world peace." But it was "not a Pax Americana enforced on the world by American weapons of war. Not the peace of the grave or the security of the slave." This was to be "not merely peace in our time but peace for all time." Kennedy hoped that the Soviets would adopt a more enlightened attitude. It was also essential that "[we] reexamine our own attitude—as individuals and as a nation—for our attitude is as essential as theirs....As Americans, we find communism profoundly repugnant as a negation of personal freedom and dignity. But we can still hail the Russian people for their many achievements—in science and space, in economic and industrial growth, in culture and in acts of courage." Kennedy warned against a Soviet-American conflict that would destroy within twenty-four hours "all we have built [and] all we have worked for." To avert such a disaster, Kennedy announced his creation of a "hot line" that would allow Washington and Moscow to talk promptly in a crisis. The other was to reach agreement on a test ban.

Although Kennedy's speech did not resonate forcefully in the United States, it received a more positive reception in the Soviet Union. Khrushchev called the speech "the best statement made by any President since Roosevelt." Though the peaceful end to the Cold War makes it difficult to understand now, public cant about Communist dangers in the 1950s and 1960s made it almost impossible for an American politician to make the sort of speech Kennedy gave. It was a tremendously bold address.

To counter assertions that he was being too soft in his dealings with the Communists, Kennedy traveled to

Europe during June 23 to July 2, 1963, to build support for test ban negotiations and provide assurances of U.S. determination to defend NATO allies against Soviet aggression. The trip was a grand triumph of public diplomacy. He spent four days each in Germany and Ireland, two days in Italy, and one in Britain. The visit to Germany, especially West Berlin, was memorable. Three-fifths of the city's population turned out to see and hear the president.

He did not disappoint them. After visiting the Berlin Wall, which "shocked and appalled" him, he spoke to a million people gathered in front of the city hall, "a sea of human faces chanting 'Kenne-dy,' 'Kenne-dy.'" In his address, which stirred the crowd to almost hysterical outbursts of approval, Kennedy declared, "Ich bin ein Berliner" ("I am a Berliner"). He decried the Communist oppression of East Germans by declaring that those who didn't understand the differences between the free world and the Communist world or doubted that Communism was an evil system or believed it possible to work with the Communists should come to Berlin. Later that day, in more measured remarks at the Free University of Berlin, he tried to "make it clear that we are not hostile to any people or system, providing they chose their own destiny without interfering with the free choices of others." As he flew out of Berlin, he told Ted Sorensen, his speechwriter, "We'll never have another day like this as long as we live."

In Ireland, he struck idealistic notes that thrilled his audiences. "Modern economics, weaponry and communications have made us realize more than ever that we are one human family and this one planet is our home." He quoted George Bernard Shaw on the influence of the Irish: "Speaking as an Irishman, [Shaw] summed up an approach to life: Other people ... 'see things and ... say: Why? ... But I dream things that never were—and I say: Why not?' "

Kennedy's prestige reached a new high. He used his standing to press ahead with a test ban agreement. The Soviets were entirely agreeable: One of their negotiators said that now that both sides had felt "the breath of death" in the missile crisis, it was time for them to cooperate. Although the Soviets would not sign on to a comprehensive treaty favored by the United States, they were eager to commit themselves to limited bans covering the atmosphere, outer space, and underwater. Within ten days of a U.S. delegation's arrival in Moscow, a treaty was signed. When Averill Harriman, America's chief delegate, told Khrushchev at a reception celebrating the completion of the treaty that he was going to a track meet, Khrushchev exclaimed, "It is better to have this kind of race than the arms race."

When conservative senators and military chiefs raised objections to Senate ratification of the treaty, Kennedy spoke to the nation. In the eighteen years since World War II, he said, the United States and the Soviet Union had talked past each other, producing "only darkness, discord, or disillusion." This fog of gloom threatened to turn into a conflict unlike any before in history—a war that, in less than sixty minutes, "could wipe out more than three hundred million Americans, European, and Russians, as well as untold numbers elsewhere. And the survivors, as Chairman Khrushchev warned the Communist Chinese, 'the survivors would envy the dead.'" But now, "a shaft of light [has] cut into the darkness.... For the first time, an agreement has been reached on bringing the forces of nuclear destruction under international control."

The pressure to approve the agreement overwhelmed its opponents. A Harris poll published on September 1, 1963, showed 81 percent of Americans backing the pact. "I don't see any political mileage in opposing the treaty," one Republican senator declared. He predicted Senate approval. He was right. On September 24, the Senate overwhelmingly endorsed the agreement with a vote of eighty to nineteen.

While the treaty did not mean the end of the international arms race for nuclear weapons—it did not deter

China, France, India, Israel, North Korea, and Pakistan from developing them—it did mark a pause in the Cold War tensions that had seemed to make a global conflict all too likely. The treaty, as Kennedy publicly acknowledged, "will not resolve all conflicts, or cause the Communist to forego their ambitions, or eliminate the dangers of war. It will not reduce our need for arms or allies.... But it is an important first step—a step toward peace—a step toward reason—a step away from war." In this, he was correct. The treaty—the first significant arms control agreement between the United States and the Soviet Union—was a milestone in the ultimately successful forty-five-year struggle to prevent the Cold War from turning into an all-out conflict that devastated the planet. And the treaty gave hope to millions of people who believed, with Kennedy, that humankind had to do away with nuclear war or war would do away with humankind. The treaty created an imperishable conviction that Kennedy might bring the Cold War to a peaceful conclusion.

At the same time that Kennedy tried to ease international tensions that could lead to war, he struggled to find the means to reduce racial strife at home. Because he saw no chance to drive a civil rights bill through Congress that would meet growing black demands for an end to racial segregation and equal treatment under the law, Kennedy initially relied on executive actions to reduce the barriers African Americans faced in casting votes, winning jobs, and gaining equal access to places of public accommodation, especially across the South, where segregation was legally and socially the accepted norm.

In the first two years of his term, Kennedy's limited actions fell well short of what black leaders expected. King believed Kennedy lacked the "moral passion" to battle for equal rights and would do no more than reach "aggressively" for "the limited goal of token integration." Although Kennedy had promised to integrate federally financed public housing with a stroke of the pen, his failure to act made his administration seem "timid and reluctant to put its full weight behind civil rights legislation." A battle over integrating interstate transportation added to feelings that Kennedy was more rhetoric than action. When the Freedom Riders, thirteen young black and white civil rights activists, boarded buses in Washington, D.C., for a trip to New Orleans through Virginia, the Carolinas, Georgia, and Alabama, it provoked segregationists to attack them. The White House tried to convince the young people to call off their trip. Although Kennedy sent administration representatives south to protect the riders, it was seen as a token gesture that skirted the fundamental issue of segregated interstate travel.

When Bobby Kennedy asked civil rights leaders for a "cooling off" period, James Farmer of the Congress of Racial Equality said: "Negroes have been cooling off for a hundred years" and would be "in a deep freeze if they cooled any further." King told *Time,* "Wait, means 'Never.'" King also complained that this was an administration that didn't "understand the social revolution going on in the world, and therefore they don't understand what we're doing."

Black activists across the South forced Kennedy's hand. In August 1962, civil rights workers launched a concerted effort to challenge the segregation laws of the southwest Georgia city of Albany. These activists were met with violence, as were black churches in Mississippi, which segregationists burned as centers of voting rights agitation. In September, when James Meredith, a black twenty-eight-year-old air force veteran, tried to enter the all-white University of Mississippi, this provoked a crisis between the White House and the governor of Mississippi, who refused to follow a court order mandating Meredith's enrollment. A televised speech by Kennedy urging the peaceful integration of the university and the presence of five hundred federal marshals were not enough to prevent violence that cost two lives and numerous injuries. With the help of federalized National Guard troops, Meredith was enrolled, and Kennedy gained standing with civil rights activists and the public in general for having taken a firm stand in the crisis.

But it couldn't stem the momentum of the civil rights crisis, which reached a new crescendo in April 1963 in Birmingham, Alabama. King and the SCLC saw the city as one of the most racist communities in the South. A nonviolent assault on its segregated laws and mores seemed certain to focus fresh national attention on the injustices suffered by blacks across the region. Peaceful demonstrations by young blacks brought attacks by the city's police using dogs that bit several demonstrators and firemen using high-pressure fire hoses that knocked marchers down and tore off their clothes. The television images broadcast across the country and around the world graphically showed out-of-control racists abusing innocent young advocates of civil rights. Kennedy, looking at a picture on the front page of the *New York Times* and television news coverage of a dog lunging to bite a teenager on the stomach, said that these images made him "sick."

Kennedy tried to find a compromise to the "spectacle which was seriously damaging the reputation of both Birmingham and the country." He feared that the overseas coverage of the crisis was damaging America's image in the Third World, where it was locked in competition with Moscow for influence. A White House–negotiated arrangement to improve the lives of Birmingham's blacks fell apart when members of the Ku Klux Klan bombed King's brother's home and a black motel, touching off a riot in the city's black ghetto and threatening to turn southern cities with large black populations into strongholds of rebellion that could threaten the civic peace. "The passivity and nonviolence of American Negroes could never again be taken for granted," two experts on southern race relations said.

To bring peace to Birmingham meant dealing with Alabama governor George Wallace, who had promised segregation now, segregation tomorrow, segregation forever. In a televised speech to the country on May 12, 1963, Kennedy promised to control domestic violence and "the fundamental right of all citizens to be accorded equal treatment and opportunity."

The dangers to public tranquility resurfaced within days, when Wallace defied a federal court order to integrate the University of Alabama, the last remaining segregated state university in the nation. The episode convinced Kennedy that he had to take bolder action to reduce the prospect of race wars across the South. Kennedy now saw the white southerners as "hopeless, they'll never reform," he said privately. "The people of the South haven't done anything about integration for a hundred years, and when an outsider interferes, they tell him to get out; they'll take care of it themselves, which they won't." It was time, he declared, to be less concerned about white southerners' feelings.

Kennedy now decided that he would have to ask Congress for a comprehensive civil rights law that would compel desegregation in all places of public accommodation. On June 10, responding to another clash with Wallace, Kennedy made a televised national address that was partly delivered extemporaneously.

It was one of his best speeches—a heartfelt appeal on behalf of a moral cause. It included several memorable lines calling on the country to honor its finest traditions. "We are confronted primarily with a moral issue," he said.

> It is as old as the scriptures and is as clear as the American Constitution. The heart of the question is whether all Americans are to be afforded equal rights and equal opportunities.... One hundred years have passed since President Lincoln freed the slaves, yet their heirs, their grandsons, are not fully free. They are not yet freed from the bonds of injustice. They are not yet freed from social and economic oppression. And this Nation, for all its hopes and all its boasts, will not be fully free until all its citizens are free.... Now the time has come for this Nation to fulfill its promise.... The fires of frustration and discord are burning in every city, North and South, where legal remedies are not at hand, and our task, our obligation, is to make that revolution, that change, peaceful and constructive for all. Next week I shall ask the Congress of the United States to act, to make a commitment it has not

fully made in this century to the proposition that race has no place in American life or law.

The following week, on June 19, Kennedy asked for the enactment of the most far-reaching civil rights bill in American history. The proposed law would ensure any citizen with a sixth-grade education the right to vote and would eliminate discrimination in all places of public accommodation—hotels, restaurants, amusement facilities, and retail establishments. Kennedy described the basis for such legislation as clearly consistent with the Fourteenth Amendment's equal protection clause, the Fifteenth Amendment's right of citizens to vote regardless of race or color, and federal control of interstate commerce. Yet the bill was anything but certain of enactment.

At the same time that Kennedy was wrestling with problems at home and in Cuba and Europe, he worried about Communist aggression in Southeast Asia, especially in South Vietnam, where an insurgency supported by North Vietnam's Communist regime in Hanoi seemed likely to topple Ngo Dinh Diem's pro-Western government unless Washington bolstered his rule. Recalling France's defeat in Vietnam, Kennedy was reluctant to offer more than financial and technical assistance. In 1961, he told advisers that before he would consider sending ground forces into the country, he wanted "indigenous forces used to the maximum" and intended to "use air and sea power to the maximum" before he would consider introducing infantry units. America's military involvement was to be a last resort.

The conventional wisdom in Washington was that the United States could not afford to abandon Vietnam: It would mean losing "not merely a crucial piece of real estate, but the faith that the U.S. has the will and the capacity to deal with the Communist offensive in that area." While not disputing the importance of holding the line against a Communist advance in Southeast Asia, Kennedy was profoundly skeptical about an overt American military response. He told the historian Arthur Schlesinger, Jr., "They [the U.S. military] want a force of American troops. They say it's necessary in order to restore confidence and restore morale.... The troops will march in; the bands will play; the crowds will cheer; and in four days everyone will have forgotten. Then we will be told we have to send in more troops. It's like taking a drink. The effect wears off, and you have to take another." He believed that if the conflict in Vietnam "were ever converted into a white man's war, we would lose the way the French had lost a decade earlier."

For all Kennedy's reluctance, international and domestic pressures persuaded him to commit new U.S. resources to

Vietnam. After the defeat at the Bay of Pigs, Khrushchev's uncompromising rhetoric in Vienna, the construction of the Berlin Wall, and a Soviet nuclear buildup, Kennedy believed that allowing Vietnam to collapse was too politically injurious to America's international standing and too likely to provoke destructive domestic opposition like that over China after the collapse of Chiang Kai-shek's Nationalist government in 1949. The result was an increase in U.S. military advisers in Vietnam from about eight hundred to over sixteen thousand during the next two years.

Kennedy was especially concerned to assure that the journalists in Saigon did not generate stories that would agitate White House opponents into demanding that he expand the war effort to save Vietnam from a Communist takeover. Kennedy also feared that news stories describing U.S. military actions in Vietnam would increase tensions with Hanoi, Peking, and Moscow and difficulties with the Soviet Union in reaching agreements on Southeast Asia, Germany, and arms control. In November 1961, Rusk cabled the Saigon embassy: "Do not give other than routine cooperation to correspondents on coverage current military activities in Vietnam. No comment at all on classified activities." At press conferences in 1962, when asked about Vietnam, Kennedy consistently played down the

United States' activities there, refusing to acknowledge that U.S. forces had entered into an undeclared war. In 1963, when David Halberstam, *New York Times* correspondent in Saigon, reported America's stumbling efforts in Vietnam, Kennedy asked *Times* publisher Arthur Sulzberger to recall Halberstam from Saigon. Sulzberger refused, and Kennedy was left to worry all the more that reports of military failure in Vietnam would stimulate increased pressure on him to expand America's role in the conflict.

With the war going badly and South Vietnam increasingly threatened with a Communist takeover, Kennedy came under pressure to support a military coup against Diem's government. John Kenneth Galbraith, his ambassador to India, urged him to withdraw U.S. support from Diem. Galbraith did not think Diem could effectively lead South Vietnam and thought it a cliché that there was no alternative to Diem. He joked, "Nothing succeeds like successors." When Henry Cabot Lodge, the U.S. ambassador in Saigon, weighed in with similar advice, Kennedy reluctantly signed off on a coup. He worried that if it failed, the United States would be blamed and "we could lose our entire position in Southeast Asia overnight." But Kennedy had lost control of events in Saigon: On November 1, South Vietnamese generals announced the formation of a new government without Diem. On the morning of November 2, Diem, who asked the generals to let him leave the country, was assassinated. They feared that he might set up a government in exile that would challenge the legitimacy of their new regime.

The assassination shook Kennedy, who recorded a statement of regret for future use by historians. "The coup in Saigon...culminated three months of conversations about a coup, conversations that divided the government here and in Saigon....I feel that we [at the White House] must bear a good deal of responsibility for it." He regretted giving his approval for a coup "without a roundtable conference at which McNamara and [General Maxwell] Taylor [head of the Joint Chiefs] could have presented their views....I was shocked by the death of Diem"— Kennedy believed Diem had deserved better from South Vietnam. "The question now is whether the generals can stay together and build a stable government."

Kennedy would never find out. Three weeks later, on November 22, 1963, he was assassinated in Dallas, where he had gone on a political fence-mending trip. Lee Harvey Oswald, his killer, was a ne'er-do-well leftist radical who had spent some time in the Soviet Union and apparently believed he was striking a retaliatory blow for Kennedy's anti-Castro Cuban policies. When Jack Ruby, an unsavory Dallas night club operator, shot and killed Oswald in the garage of a Dallas police station where he was being held prior to appearing at a court hearing, the country concluded that Kennedy's death had been the work of more than one man.

Although the Warren Commission—the government's inquiry into the assassination, headed by Chief Justice Earl Warren—described Oswald in its September 1964 report as the lone killer, a majority of Americans have never accepted this conclusion. To be sure, the commission's failure to ferret out and disclose CIA assassination plots against Castro or to reveal and condemn the FBI for inattentiveness to Oswald raised questions later about the reliability of its evidence and judgment. But in December 1963, even before the commission published its findings, 52 percent of the populace said they saw "some group or element" behind the assassination. By 1967, the belief in a conspiracy had risen to 64 percent. Now, almost five decades after Kennedy's killing, some 70 percent of Americans continue to believe that Oswald was the instrument of a group that wanted Kennedy out of the way.

The fact that none of the conspiracy theorists have been able to offer convincing evidence of their suspicions does not seem to trouble many people. The plausibility of a conspiracy is less important to them than the implausibility of someone as inconsequential as Oswald having the wherewithal to kill someone as consequential—as powerful and well guarded—as Kennedy. To accept that an act of random violence by an obscure malcontent could bring down a president of the United States is to acknowledge a chaotic, disorderly world. To believe that Oswald killed Kennedy is to concede, as former *New York Times* columnist Anthony Lewis said, "that in this life there is often tragedy without reason."

Kennedy's assassination provoked not only conspiracy theories but also an extraordinary public attachment to his memory. Almost fifty years after his death, Americans consistently rate Kennedy as one of the great presidents in U.S. history. Fifty-two percent of respondents in a 1975 Gallup poll ranking presidents put Kennedy first, ahead of Lincoln and Franklin Roosevelt; ten years later, Kennedy remained number one in the opinion of 56 percent of respondents. A poll released on Presidents' Day in February 1999 declared Lincoln the greatest of our presidents, with George Washington, Kennedy, Ronald Reagan, and Bill Clinton tied for second. In 2000, Kennedy topped the list, followed by Lincoln, Franklin Roosevelt, and Reagan. Currently he continues to be identified by most Americans as one of the five greatest presidents along with Washington, Lincoln, Franklin Roosevelt, and Reagan.

The assassination and Kennedy's martyrdom no doubt remain the most important factors in perpetuating high public regard for his leadership and importance as a president. But this alone can not explain his popularity. McKinley, twice-elected and popular when he was assassinated in 1901, is now an all but forgotten president. The advent of television, which captured Kennedy's youthful appearance, good looks, charm, wit, and rhetorical idealism and hope, has also contributed to his continuing appeal. In addition, his sensible behavior in response to the Cuban Missile Crisis and the civil rights struggles recommend him to Americans and encourage a belief that had he lived, the country might have avoided the sorts of problems it suffered under LBJ and Richard Nixon.

How, then, to assess Kennedy's abbreviated presidency?

The domestic record of Kennedy's thousand days is distinctly limited. On civil rights, the greatest issue of the early 1960s, he was a cautious leader. Despite executive orders and federal lawsuits opposing southern segregation, he was slow to recognize the extent of the social revolution fostered by King and African Americans. It took crises in Mississippi and particularly in Alabama to persuade him to put a landmark civil rights bill before Congress in June 1963.

None of Kennedy's major reform initiatives—the tax cut, federal aid to education, Medicare, or civil rights—became law during his time in office. Yet all his significant reform proposals, including plans for a housing agency and a major assault on poverty, which he discussed in 1961 and 1963, came to fruition under LBJ. Johnson, of course, deserves considerable credit for these reforms. He won passage of the tax cut and civil rights bills in 1964; anti-poverty, federal aid to education, Medicare, and voting rights laws in 1965; and statutes creating cabinet-level transportation and housing and urban development agencies in 1966.

Johnson's enactment of Kennedy's reform agenda testifies to their shared wisdom about the national well-being. Part of Kennedy's legacy should be an understanding that he proposed major domestic reforms that have had an enduring constructive impact on the country. No one should deny LBJ credit in winning passage of so many bills in the reform program he called the Great Society. Nevertheless, it is arguable that Kennedy would have made similar gains in a second term. It is doubtful that Kennedy would have been as aggressive as LBJ in expanding the reform program set before Congress in 1965 and 1966, but the major bills pending from Kennedy's term would all have found their way into the law books. The most important of the Great Society measures deserve to be described as Kennedy-Johnson achievements.

Foreign affairs were the principal concerns of Kennedy's presidency. The Peace Corps and the Alliance for Progress, which aimed to use American expertise to raise Third World living standards, and the Apollo program, which excited hopes of future space exploration, were significant measures of his foreign policy performance. The Peace Corps and his commitment to land a man on the Moon were great successes; the Alliance was an exercise in unrealized hopes. All three programs initially generated great enthusiasm, at home and abroad, where they were seen as representative of America at its best—a generous advanced nation promoting a better life for less fortunate peoples around the globe.

Kennedy's focus on Cuba, relations with the Soviet Union, and actions in Vietnam are telling measures of his presidential effectiveness. The Bay of Pigs failure and the repeated discussions of how to topple Castro that followed show Kennedy at his worst. But the almost universal praise for his restraint and accommodation in the Missile Crisis, followed by secret explorations of détente with Havana, more than make up for his initial errors of judgment. Indeed, a second Kennedy term might have bought a resolution of the unproductive tensions with Castro and perhaps foreclosed fifty years of Cuban-American antagonism.

Vietnam, which became America's worst foreign policy nightmare in the twelve years after Kennedy's death, is a source of sharp debate between critics and admirers of his leadership. His increase of military advisers to over sixteen thousand and his agreement to the coup are described as setting the course for America's later large-scale involvement in the Vietnam War. Johnson continually justified his escalation of America's role in the conflict by emphasizing that he was simply following Kennedy's lead.

A close reading of the record suggests that Kennedy had every wish to keep Vietnam out of the Soviet-Chinese Communist orbit but was unwilling to pay any price or bear any burden for the freedom of Saigon from Communist control. His fear of turning the war into a struggle on the same scale as the Korean War and of getting trapped in a war that demanded ever more U.S. resources became reasons in 1963 for him to plan reductions of U.S. military personnel in South Vietnam. His eagerness to mute press criticism of America's failure to defeat Communism in Southeast Asia also rested on his resistance to escalating U.S. involvement in the struggle. No one can prove, of course, what Kennedy would have done about Vietnam between 1964 and 1968. His actions and statements, however, are suggestive of a carefully managed stand-down from the sort of involvement that occurred under LBJ.

By November 1963, Kennedy had established himself as a strong foreign policy leader. After facing down Khrushchev in the missile crisis and overcoming Soviet and U.S. military and Senate resistance to a test ban treaty,

Kennedy had much greater credibility as a defender of the national security than LBJ had. It gave Kennedy more freedom to convince people at home and abroad that staying clear of large-scale military intervention in Vietnam was in the best interest of the United States. No one can say with any certainty that two full Kennedy terms would have eased the Cold War between the United States and the Soviet Union. But it is certainly imaginable.

The sudden ending of Kennedy's life and presidency has left us with tantalizing might-have-beens. Yet, even setting these aside and acknowledging some missed opportunities and false steps, it must be acknowledged that his thousand days spoke to the country's better angels, inspired visions of a less divisive nation and world, and demonstrated that America was still the last best hope of humankind.

The Kennedy legacy, of course, would not end with John F. Kennedy's death. For the next four and a half years, Robert Kennedy would take center stage in American politics—up to and including his bid for the presidency in 1968, which ended with his tragic assassination. Ted Kennedy would assume leadership of the family and use his Massachusetts Senate seat to become the Democratic Party's leading liberal spokesperson. His death after forty-six years as a senator and his son Patrick's decision in 2010 not to run for another term as congressman from Rhode Island marked the end, at least for a time, of the political prominence of the Kennedy dynasty, whose scions held elected office in Washington for fifty-two years, from 1947 to 2009.

Sources

Citations for all the quotations in this book can be found in the notes to *An Unfinished Life: John F. Kennedy, 1917–1963* (2003), from which this brief life is drawn.

The sources for *An Unfinished Life,* from which this brief life is drawn, were numerous manuscript collections, tape recordings, oral histories, interviews, conversations, and newspaper and magazine articles. Much of this material is housed in the John F. Kennedy Library in Boston. More detailed identification of these sources can be found in the notes section of *An Unfinished Life.*

The principal books that were of use in writing *An Unfinished Life* were Irving Bernstein, *Promises Kept: John F. Kennedy's New Frontier* (1991); Michael R. Beschloss, *The Crisis Years: Kennedy and Khrushchev, 1960–1963* (1991); James G. Blight and David A. Welch, *On the Brink: Americans and Soviets Reexamine the Cuban Missile Crisis* (1989); Taylor Branch,

Parting the Waters: America in the King Years, 1954–1963 (1988); Peter Collier and David Horowitz, *The Kennedys: An America Drama* (1984); Robert Dallek, *Flawed Giant: Lyndon Johnson and His Times, 1961–1973* (1998); Lawrence Freedman, *Kennedy's Wars: Berlin, Cuba, Laos, and Vietnam* (2000); Aleksandr Fursenko and Timothy Naftali, *"One Hell of a Gamble": Khrushchev, Castro, and Kennedy, 1958–1964* (1997); George Gallup, *The Gallup Poll: Public Opinion, 1935–1971,* 3 vols. (1972); William C. Gibbons, *The U.S. Government and the Vietnam War,* pt. 2, *1961–1964* (1984); James N. Giglio, *The Presidency of John F. Kennedy* (1991); Gordon M. Goldstein, *Lessons in Disaster: McGeorge Bundy and the Path to War in Vietnam* (2008); Doris Kearns Goodwin, *The Fitzgeralds and the Kennedys* (1987); Edwin O. Guthman, *We Band of Brothers: A Memoir of Robert F. Kennedy* (1971); Edwin O. Guthman and Jeffrey Shulman, eds., *Robert Kennedy: In His Own Words* (1988); David Halberstam, *The Making of a Quagmire: America and Vietnam* (1988); Nigel Hamilton, *Reckless Youth* (1992); David Kaiser, *American Tragedy: Kennedy, Johnson, and the Origins of the Vietnam War* (2000); Montague Kern, Patricia W. Levering, and Ralph B. Levering, *The Kennedy Crises: The Press, the Presidency, and Foreign Policy* (1983); Peter Kornbluth, ed., *Bay of Pigs Declassified: The Secret CIA Report on the Invasion of Cuba* (1998); Lawrence Leamer, *The Kennedy Men,1901–1963* (2001); Evelyn Lincoln, *My Twelve Years with John F. Kennedy* (1965); Robert S. McNamara, *In Retrospect: The Tragedy and Lessons of Vietnam* (1995); William

Manchester, *The Death of a President* (1967); Ernest R. May and Philip D. Zelikow, eds., *The Kennedy Tapes: Inside the White House during the Cuban Missile Crisis* (1997); Timothy Naftali, ed., *The Presidential Recordings: John F. Kennedy: The Great Crises,* vol. 2, *September–October 21, 1962* (2001); John M. Newman, *JFK and Vietnam* (1992); Lawrence O'Brien, *No Final Victories* (1974); Kenneth P. O'Donnell and David F. Powers, *"Johnny We Hardly Knew Ye"* (1970); Herbert Parmet, *The Struggles of John F. Kennedy* (1980); Herbert Parmet, *The Presidency of John F. Kennedy* (1984); Geoffrey Perrault, *Jack: Nothing Like Him in the World* (2001); Gerald Posner, *Case Closed: Lee Harvey Oswald and the Assassination of JFK* (1993); Stephen G. Rabe, *"The Most Dangerous Area in the World": John F. Kennedy Confronts Communist Revolution in Latin America* (1999); Richard Reeves, *President John F. Kennedy: Profile of Power* (1993); Thomas C. Reeves, *A Question of Character: A Life of John F. Kennedy* (1991); Dean Rusk, *As I Saw It* (1990); William J. Rust, *Kennedy in Vietnam* (1985); Pierre Salinger, *With Kennedy* (1966); Arthur Schlesinger, Jr., *A Thousand Days* (1965); Arthur Schlesinger, Jr., *Robert Kennedy and His Times* (1978); Glenn T. Seaborg, *Kennedy, Khrushchev, and the Test Ban* (1981); Deborah Shapley, *Promise and Power: The Life and Times of Robert McNamara* (1993); Theodore C. Sorensen, *Kennedy* (1966); Maxwell D. Taylor, *Swords and Plowshares* (1972); Evan Thomas, *Robert Kennedy: His Life* (2002); Janet Travell, *Office Hours: Day and Night: The Autobiography of Janet Travell, M.D.* (1968); Theodore

H. White, *The Making of the President, 1960* (2010 ed.); Garry Wills, *The Kennedy Imprisonment: A Meditation on Power* (1981); Harris Wofford, *Of Kennedys and Kings* (1980); Peter Wyden, *The Bay of Pigs: The Untold Story* (1979); Peter Wyden, *Wall: The Inside Story of Divided Berlin* (1989); Philip Zelikow and Ernest May, eds., *The Presidential Recordings: John F. Kennedy: The Great Crises,* vol. 3, *October 22–28, 1962* (2001); Peter S. Canellos, ed., *Last Lion: The Fall and Rise of Ted Kennedy* (2009); Ted Sorensen, *Counselor: Life at the Edge of History* (2008); Edward M. Kennedy, *True Compass: A Memoir* (2009).